Radio & Other Miracles

Radio & Other Miracles

Terrance Cox

Catherine Hunter, Editor

Cover design by Terry Gallagher/Doowah Design.
Author photo by Stephen Dominick.

We acknowledge the financial support of The Canada Council for the Arts and the Manitoba Arts Council for our publishing program.

Printed and bound in Canada by AGMV Marquis Imprimeur.

Canadian Cataloguing in Publication Data

Cox, Terrance
      Radio & other miracles

Poems.
ISBN 0-921833-82-2
      I. Title.

PS8555.O983R3 2001   C811'.54   C2001-902551-3
PR9199.3.C673R3 2001

Signature Edtions
P.O. Box 206, RPO Corydon , Winnipeg, MB Canada R3M 3S7

Acknowledgements

Many of the poems in *Radio & Other Miracles* were published in earlier versions—indeed, sometimes much earlier versions—in literary journals. My thanks to the editors and staff of the following for encouragement and prescient acumen:

> *Antigonish Review, BC Monthly, Border Crossings,*
> *Dalhousie Review, Descant, The Fiddlehead,*
> *Grain, Lunatic Gazette, Mamashee, New Quarterly,*
> *Northern Light, Northward Journal, Origins,*
> *Pierian Spring, Prism International, Quarry,*
> *Queen's Quarterly, Wascana Review*

Other poems included here also appear on the "spoken word with music" CD, *Local Scores*, published by Cyclops Press.

Many of these poems are themselves gestures of tribute, with dedications attached. Thanks again to all those thus named.

Beyond those debts are more I owe to others, here acknowledged, for their extraordinary and sustaining presence: Arleen Bush, Nick Baxter-Moore, Sarah Cooper, Jeff Hale, Clive Holden, and Matthew Poulakakis.

Especial thanks to Catherine Hunter for exemplary editorship.

Table of Contents

I

Gut Scrapes and Reel

Schottische for Maggie
(for Margaret Garland, 1896-1985)

Off Mariposa stage in Québécois
accent, an anecdote
gets told of Saturday nights
in long-ago winters how
Marcel Messervier's Allstars'
accordion & fiddle rivalled
hockey for radio dial

that practice of *pays d'en haut*
pooled home & visitors' sets
to tune in both & do-si-do
kitchen to front parlour
fiddles to *les Canadiens*

Up north, almost as far
on hardscrabble hundred acres
this side of border, dirty 30s
thru second war, resound
same reels & schottisches
off cabinet in parlour that
scrimped egg-money bought
tho boys upstairs with crystal set
are rooting for the Leafs

Grandmother Maggie—
she of up-north acres
& egg-money radio—
sure could jig & schottische
despite crippled hip
& who, I bet you, knows
name of every piece that
band in Allstars' tribute plays—

while out under midsummer's silver
stage lights & full moon
old-time tunes astonish
thousands of young ears—

in North Bay hospital this night
at eighty-nine, lies dying

In friends' small circle, we raise
wine in paper-cup salute
to Maggie, who, tho teetotal,
excuses wickedness in grandsons
& does, I hope, accept
tribute in proper spirit

I call out a dedication:
Next schottische for Maggie!

mid which gesture making
I collapse, fall to knees & tears

& can no longer hear
fiddles & accordion
on stage at Mariposa or
over scrimped-for radio
pride of place in parlour

only keening silence
& I know

Icarus Otherwise, South Himsworth
(for Stan Garland)

Stan, in historical present
of that August he turns twelve,
poises intensely at edge
of pre-Cambrian cliff, peers
down steep igneous slope, sees
how test flight might, arcing, soar:

fleet over scrub brush & eskers
storming ramshackle barn

swoop up at stump fences
curdle milk of cows in pasture
scare chickens out of coop

skim, in descent, big toe
in whisky-coloured creek

Stan, for seventy-eleventh time,
reviews aeronautic
principles & handiwork
put, in chores-done hours,
to wings of twelve-foot span

to each glued wood-scrap
strut & flour-bag panel—
faded brand name markings
as squadron's roundels—pauses

cusp of caution, saying
Maybe try tomorrow, hears
young sister Winnie, his
tag-along ground crew, voice
doubts, out loud,
he owns to in silence

You'll hurt yourself, she says
& presto, he launches off

Stan, in upside-down
flashback, some six years before:

showing off, in winter kitchen
new achievement of a headstand,
warned to watch out,
loses balance, flails,
legs wide open, into woodstove,
spills on self entire
black cauldron of boiling water—

about, that winter night,
to be lifted off
by Cec & Thompson, carried
out as heat to Garland's
Poultry Farm's incubator—

scalds from shin to thigh
thoroughly both legs
past skin thru muscles
deep to bone, & screams

Stan, in lengthy convalescence,
come to almost spring,
as skin turns livid scar
& muscles atrophy, refuses
even to attempt to walk
at best, infantile, will crawl

It is 1926, with traces
of lingering snowdrifts
in shady spots yet, & then

as slow crescendo comes
engine noise of first
ever monoplane to fly
skies above Garland's Farm,

hailed by all inhabitants:
chickens' flustered squawks,
roosters' crow at new age's dawn
humans, running, shouting, waving—
all but two, that is:

Maggie, stirring pots &, off
in boredom & kitchen corner
pitiful on daybed, poor Stan

To his wail that wondrous
aeroplane was, from window-less
confines, impossible to see,
Maggie barely shrugs, suggests
Best get up & walk, I guess

Devout wish defeating doubt
Stan hauls off pallet, crawls
to doorway, pulls to standing
stumbles down porch steps
hobbles halfway to barnyard
in jubilation passing measure
shouts *I see it! I see it!*

at utter of eureka
realizes that he walks,
in exultant laughter
tearfully tumbles

So subsequent loudly does
whole family whoop,
back that bushplane circles
treetop low, wave of wing salutes

Stan, in present continuous,
I hear tell his grandkids
that prototype glider
dammit, damn well flew

that for lifetime's worth
of seconds he was airborne

that, free-of-earth in '32,
he sees from on high:

hatchery & laying sheds,
Maggie outside summer kitchen

secret tree fort behind house
Cec & hired hand
in spy-apple orchard

Thompson in potato field
& well beyond to sugar bush

Seeing all this
enough for forever
before his home-forged craft
stalls, spins out & crashes

Stan, with minor scrapes
& bruises, with his
epiphanic twelve-foot wings
smashed to kindling
limps away in triumph

After overseas in Air Force
stint as ground crew mechanic
Stan works next forty years
at gas station & garage
on main street of Powassan—
a business he comes to own—
mends & tunes engines
refuels & repairs

Stan, on eightieth birthday,
tosses back two whiskies

& keeping promise to himself

executes a wobbly few
seconds' achievement
dammit, of a headstand

buggers up his shoulder
& rib muscles but good

Nine Goals in One Game

(for Sharkey Cox)

About clipping from newspaper
I am certain, remember
at age seven asking & how
Sharkey with show of reluctance
pulls from folds of wallet,
yellowed, frayed at creases,
a CP wire service
account of wondrous feat:

Nine goals! In one game!
This man in shopkeeper's apron,
who looks like Dad but older,
scored nine goals in one game

With front door glass in gothic
script that spells out
Grandpa's initials & our name
with ampersand adds "Sons"
above legend in block capitals
that reads "General Merchants"

store with false front, gingerbread
& pillars painted white—
bay window for display of goods—
stands, corner of Mill & King,
town of Powassan, for ages

has been J.W.'s long since
before Sharkey on left wing
starred for hometown Hawks—
one late 30s season
champions of Intermediate
playoffs for whole province

Slick, they say Sharkey was,
slick as oiled-back haircut:
wizard with a shoulder deke
could stickhandle like a devil
skate, if riled, like blizzard wind
had one wicked backhand

17

I never saw his telegram
call-up to the Red Wings'
pre-season camp, nor
train ticket that came later
to Detroit for a tryout

Bell above entranceway
that jangles as door opens,
creaks of floorboard slats
even a kid's weight causes,
smell of dry goods & dustbane—
a world apart, where I was
welcomed, by blood, part of:

Enormous white weigh scale
ancient black cash till
numbers on keys of shiny gold fleck
fingers have mostly worn off
hodgepodge of canned stuff
stacked on shelves behind
counter to ceiling, where hangs

upside-down, a spool of string
threaded thru eyelet on countertop
ready at Sharkey's right
to tie up parcel, wrapped
in brown paper, torn
off big roll at left—
amazing to watch
as a conjuror's trick

Good luck at cards, I learn, is
how come he's called Sharkey
Lucky at cards as I overhear
grownup relatives at gossip
At damn-all else! swears one
second cousin, twice-removed
to tsk-tsk all about & sighs
telling brief glances until
notice of Russ's kid
brings upon shushes

Centre aisle, with angled glass
three—I think—cold lockers,
Art Deco in white enamel
On other side, more Early North
Ontario hardwood counters
cheesecloth over wooden boxes
of cheddar rounds & cookies

Whole left side for dry goods—
smiled upon by Scottish lass
from far wall's big green tin
advertisement for MacDonald
"Export," plain & filtertip:

Bolts of cloth & longjohns
shoes & boots & a motif
of plaids pursued in flannel—
shirts thru mitts to parka hoods
& hunting caps with earlugs

Of such wares, one tilted sample
displays in open box & tissue
Rest of stock is all—
haphazardly of system—
wedged under counters or
high, yon & hither, on shelves
with sliding ladder to reach
highest boxes up, hard against
swirl patterns of tin ceiling

I go, every visit, straight
off back to pop cooler, one
you lift front half of metal lid
pull cream soda by its bottlecap
along slots to a thingamajig
that Sharkey's nickel opens

sit on great big padded wooden
bench with Grandpa's cronies
later sneak thru door marked "Private"
play with antique typewriter

daunt foot-worn slippery stairs
down to spooky cellar
with musty sneezy smells
& plank incline for barrels

I cannot put together Sharkey's
nine goals in one game
with his passing rest of life
as eldest after ampersand
tending J.W.'s general store:

—never married, always taking
meals at mother's table
sleeping in same bedroom,
childhood until death

—save for overseas in Air Force
'39-to-'45 & meeting
once on leave in Bournemouth
both Uncle Mick & Dad

—give or take thirty-five seasons'
weeks at hunt camp or fishing

—& shushing up for every
sudsy evening but Sundays
at Windsor Hotel or the Legion

Never once on left wing
ice of any NHL arena

Nine goals in one game!

No one speaks about
what did not happen

The Maple Sugar Breakdown

(for Thompson Garland)

Sleet & in a small city, driving
black ice streets to classes,
almost Christmas
I am transfixed by tune
on AM CBC
that in seconds transports
northward: back two decades

to Garland's farm & over
memories, so deep
snowdrifted I thought,
till then, forgotten,
that with broadcast play along

From first bar scratches
of old-time fiddle,
so well I do remember still
these sweet gut scrapes
& reel of Nipissing tune
"The Maple Sugar Breakdown":

Spile that sap. All on down we boil 'er
Maple sugar, amber golden, maple sugar

Six I am, & reins in hand,
driving horse-drawn sleigh, yell
"haw" then "gee," as Uncle
Thompson lets me, for real, think
I, thru bush, bust trail at twilight

Swear I taste sweetness, still
warm around kitchen table
hear his fiddle
with cousins eat fill
of taffy-pulled syrup
we poured on snowbank

Song made froze feet tap,
toes thaw, feel—gut scrapes
& reel of Nipissing tune
"The Maple Sugar Breakdown":

Deep tap so. Bucketfuls to gather
Maple sugar, crystal amber, maple sugar

August last, thirty plus, I learn,
twice myself now uncle,
that tune I cherish
after Thompson is not
ours alone, but classic
late 40s piece by Ward Allan—
plays, on tape, right now,
by the Townsends

As lilacs waft
spring up off Sherbourne
for Dylan, my nephew,
Meghan, my niece, I wish
memories of seldom uncle,

songs warm & pure
& half as strong as
vats set to boil & Thompson's
fiddle's right gut scrapes
& reel of Nipissing tune
"The Maple Sugar Breakdown":

Tin pails topped. Off to vat we haul 'er
Sing this song, sing at fullest measure
Reap March flow of winter's sweetwater:
Maple sugar, crystal amber, maple sugar

Unheard Melodies

Let's assume Keats's mute
pottery pipers blow
Agora hits, long gone missing:
Homeric lyre tunes, adapted
modal "goat song," that spring's score
from rites of Dionysus

Let's imagine like fantastic
phantom bands perform
fabled silenced music, other ages:

gutsy harp & tabor, theme & variations
on harmony of sagas

psaltery & hautboys incidentals
as from Globe's gallery graced
scenic changes—sackbut for alarums

catalogue guitar & broomstick
bo diddley do Delta
blues before it got a name

Buddy Bolden's preterhuman
trumpet, solos with sextet
lineup as per famous photo

Eccentric wish in so august a
company & awesome canon
I request my Uncle Thompson's
round & square dance band
Trout Creek or environs
Saturday night after chores
shortly after second war:

Thompson, clarinet, sax & fiddle
buxom girl singer, kid tenor
who does also dance calls
adept fellow on whatever piano
church hall or fairground's pavilion has

with most of requisite keys
if not a recent tuning

Give guitarist Gibson archtop
& five-string banjo to flail
I doubt there was a drum kit
—perhaps a standup bass—
can almost hear accordion

No dancer-to & witness I
can these days ask remembers
repertoire of Thompson's band

In happy accident of absent fact
I listen to as follows:

schottische, segue to foxtrot
strathsbey, jitterbug, reel
à la main left to low-down shuffle

honky-tonk off blue-noted drone
breakdowns, jive & Bob Wills
Don Messer to Artie Shaw—

music to square
terpsichorean circle
do-si-do & vice versa
enough to raise our dead

Whatever Uncle Thompson's
outfit really did play was,
in overwhelming likelihood,
not at all so hot—
a tad this side of sweet—

&, if so,
I concur with Keats

Thompson's Impromptu

No account survives to tell
why at Garland Poultry Farm—

with Cec & Maggie getting on
retired to Trout Creek
& Thompson now in charge—

one early 50s autumn day
all the roosters
hove off high up trees

Variants of tale concur
on barnyard ordinariness
of roosters, differ on
numbers & how high

up in windbreak shade trees
about old summer kitchen
of what, a shame, soon was
derelicted farmhouse

All agree on moral laxness
since repeal of Garland Poultry's
hold to Protestant ethos

One pictures how so graceless
cockerels flew—
with frantic squawks
& stubby-wingéd flurry—

well imagines as comic
collective bantams' perch & hears
cacophony of sunset crowing

panic as silly fowls discover
vertigo & mental challenges
they simply are not equal to

Enter scene, brother Stan
down dozen miles from Powassan
dirty garage workday done
heartburn from a gobbled supper

not a little lately anxious
at fair-haired elder brother's
laisser-faire approach to farming

finding aforementioned
roosters & Thompson
at summer kitchen table—

fiddle under lantern chin
flailing horsetail bow—

huge great grin on his face

Seems to Stan an urgency
applies to situation
calling, before darkness falls,
for ladders & a rescue

Stan, I know, is still annoyed
that Thompson only laughs
by gaslight plays a parcel
of reels & jigs & offers—

as balm from first-born son
to so hard-working brother—

a grand new tune
his fingers found that day

I need to hear my uncle
Thompson's impromptu
fiddle tune that so amazed

all those roosters
hove off high up trees

keep trying here to write it

II

Distant Correspondence

A Radio of One's Own

*"...unmistakably, the three sharp clicks corresponding to three dots
sounded in my ear."*
—Marconi, describing the first transatlantic
radio message, received 12/12/1901, Signal Hill

Agency a squat brown bakelite
superannuated RCA
Victor table model
with smoky-yellow dial—
wanting but a dust-off
a vacuum tube or two—

distant correspondence
sounded unmistakably
in age about eleven ear:
messages that clicked

Off came hardboard back
panel with printed cautions
I ignored, exposing
innards to rig up
earphone salvaged from
defunct crystal set, & thus

down in basement bedroom
suburbs of a nowhere city
I could in splendid
privacy & pajamas
listen, lights out, undercover—

late nights as atmospherics
fool with AM signals—

pull in far-off places:

New York, New York
Boston, Massachusetts
Buffalo—all static-free

Detroit, sometimes
Chicago, not so often

By furtive hour & deft
minute adjustments
to smoky-yellow dial,
I clear-channelled bliss:
50,000 watts' worth

On freakish perfect secret
nights I could tune in:

Memphis, Tennessee
south of Texas border bandits
New Orleans only once

Doubtless, too, Signor Marconi
that December, year of '01
high upon Signal Hill
St. John's, Newfoundland
knew such awe

headset to anxious ear
hearing letter *s* in Morse
code across Atlantic
wireless

was amazed as I was
sixty years after—
still am a century since—
at miracle of radio:

out of merest air
matter

Eight Transistor

Gordie was the first
kid at West Front Public
with an eight transistor:
leatherette case, lunchbox size

Grade six & Easter over
ages left of school till summer
us guys after suppertime
hang around about his
imported plastic radio —
princes in our schoolyard

Devotees, we are
scornful of local station's
out-of-date chart:
three weeks old, its
so-called hot new singles

stuff that we have got
off by heart already—
gimmicks down, gist of lyrics—
heard off stations in the States

Maudlin dreck, much was:
with violins & "lonely" in title
singers all named Bobby
or masochistic female variants
plaintive in tremulous triplets

Overt nonsense, a lot:
rama lama pop sh-pop
purple aliens & monsters
escaped out of lab & id

Paeans to surf & California
celebrations of souped-up rod

Blooming in bland time
we wait out an interregnum

huddle-up, third & goal
yo-yo spinning, inch from sidewalk

champion this trash
in monophone as perfect
assume ourselves to be
blessed by eight transistor:

next to teeter-totter
hanging out by go-go-round
sneaking, ho-hum
incidental glances at those
grade six girls, somehow
new graced with strange
allure & auras

We spy on alien colleagues
whispering their secrets
turnabout jangling swingset:

girls who are sorta ok
girls who, by & by
en masse saunter closer
lured by Gordie's eight
transistor's invitation
to oldest dance on earth

a seesaw ride to share
grasped-onto hunches,
fine-tuning an adjustment
to hormonal static—

rise & fall & rise & fall & all
couplets & anemic backbeat—

until curfew whistle blows
or batteries wear out

We shut our playground gate
pair off for a roundabout
walk home on
a different planet

Mercury

"To be an earthman I must leave Earth"
—Milton Acorn

Even old school's meanest
teacher set aside
daybook & routine, put
black & white & frivolous
classroom tv on
for Mercury's historic
sub-orbital first flights:

missions into space that last
barely long as recess, go
never more than Colonel Glenn's
three earth orbits

fuzzy broadcasts always with
rocket science geeks
speaking acronyms
& Walter Cronkite, worried

As up to nearer heavens
homo sapiens now ventures
seeking recompense
worthy of heroic theft—

to parlay for Prometheus
his overdue release—

aboard our messenger's
projectile capsules ride
automatons in spacesuits
drones entirely under
Canaveral's control

No seat-of-pants, true pilot
steers by first step
closer stars

no freewheeling
stratospheric new Hermes

It is a leaden tale
heard thru static
earth-bound, in flat prose

I did learn, nonetheless
attentive then to Glenn's
go-rounds about us

off snowy CBS
from Vermont with
primitive video graphics

two astounding words
apropos our future
discourse with titans:

apogee

(remotest point in any arc)

& perigee

(that position nearest
earth in planetary orbit)—

two words I heard
that grade-school day
as first time ever uttered
to describe an earthling—

apogee

&

perigee

adjectives of astrophysics
applied to human vessel

February 9, 1964

(for Debbie McConnell Dalgleish)

Left-handed, I liked Paul best
I am sorry

As usual, your folks had put
by seven p.m. you & baby
sister both to bed—
there to stay & so charged
thirteen-year-old sitter—

as if sleep or school
tomorrow existed
this of all Sunday nights:
excitement topping scale
so widespread it reaches
even Cornwall—
live in black & white & soon

Come eight o'clock, you
snuck out to tv & pled
(extremely well) your case:
cited enormity
of moment, pure
aesthetics, peer status
fifty cents as bribe
begged on knees, "Puh-leez!"

Straight-A prick, those days
sort grownups liked
whole lots, of course, I
followed orders:
deaf to entreaty did not
let you watch with me
The Beatles on "Ed Sullivan"

You hid in hallway, I hope
heard, saw & thus also
can date exactly when
began big surprise of future

John was way the best
I am sorry

35

Great Strides

Always, those winters, there was
on street's end vacant lots
flooded & scraped, a public rink:

spite of waist-high plywood boards
a little too little for nevermind games
of pick-up day-long hockey, but

perfect for, sometimes, after supper
private think & skate alone

Deep in thought as ever gets
the fifteen-year-old kid, I there
skated hours, counter-clockwise

under streetlamp & singular spell
of so cool Dylan song, around, around
tracing blades' own hone

again, again, inside head reciting
"Love Minus Zero: No Limit"

Clueless, baffled, nary hint
about what those lyrics meant
I harder strode accelerating circles

until lungs & adolescent muscles
burning like furnace, fired brain
blue steel keen to apprehend:

puzzle out his words because
they sounded true, like ice

High Fidelity (85)
(for Matthew Poulakakis)

All still works, sometimes

Lots, now, twenty years away
I listen to pop records
cut back one epoch
into lunch-hours lost, awestruck
by single hits, riffing
racks for new releases
tracing bullets on the chart

As by analog, twice-over
revolve in memorial recess
before vinyl gathered gilt
when penny over stylus solved
dilemmas of dust & scratches
flawed mono on the Silvertone

I track selfsame lust
those days of acne, furtive
fondle & sha-la always love her
holding hands supposed, yeah
to be congress sung about

Spun off bargain plastic
I drink in bag rye seasons
outside high school gym
suspended fool with cohorts
too cowed to risk dance-floor
twist with fall term's flame
lest DJ spring slow drag

I parse in past imperfect
cheap powers; conjure
out of shallows these
real groovy illusions
how heavy is slight music
playthings of strange faith

I reckon time by rpm
well-passed presence
long play or large
hole in the centre

Going Over

(pour les gars de Cornwall)

Boneheads, entire bunch of us—
weekends "going over"
river to Massena—
took as given
fact we were immortal

Eight guys, stupid drunk,
crammed inside rust-bucket
speeding homeward, get
pulled over by state trooper

Smokey, after gentle roust—
false i.d. & licence check—
says "Ok, hit the road"

Smart-ass Laframboise—
before anyone can stop him—
stoops down, pounds his
fists on Interstate 37

Poulin, *maudit calice,*
in fog off St. Lawrence
guesses which way
curve ahead goes—
lets go of steering wheel,
dumb bastard, chooses
to have car decide

Carrier, as clever ploy
foiling any Customs hassle
over six-packs, hangs
head & shoulders out
boothside backseat window
fakes throwing up
then does

Mocking bark of Mohawk
dogs, we war whoop thru
St. Regis reserve

on Cornwall Island
rev up our idiocy

By far dumbest stunt
transpires on still new bridge
last leg before home
snakey, high & twisted
very late:

no traffic but ourselves
both lanes blocked
halfway across
at bridge's utmost
vertigo-inducing height—

furtive glimpses far below
of St. Lawrence's swirling
currents of black water—

us all cheering on
two imbeciles who race
heel & toe, in parallel
up along a double-arch
trestle of iron girders
a foot, at best, in width

I wake up sometimes still
from nightmares of this:

see those silhouettes
against full moon
& sulphurous cloud
from paper mill stack

hear maybe a dozen
car radios in unison
doors wide open, play
an Eric Burdon song

big hit that last summer
with chorus says that we
gotta get outta this place.

III

Perplexed to Be Here

"Layla": Theme & Variations

1   1970

In late fall's drear & nowhere
northeast off metropolis
I drive, terrified, on 401

way past posted speed
jumped by traffic frenzy
with AM's blather as
horrific complement
to this controlled-access
chaos in sixteen lanes

I, white-knuckled, barrel thru
until—unlikely as the chance of
roadside wildflowers
or birdsong bursting forth
mid toxicity & concrete—

there speaks a human voice
that, left field, out of format
allows as how not loving
this song, up next, means
"Man, you know nothing!"

& then he plays "Layla"—
whole, more-than-seven-minutes,
Derek & the Dominos,
two-disc, eponymous album,
certified version

By bless of last fading lilt
I descend Don Valley
fearless & amazed

Afterwards, that human voice
reverts to hype & jingle

as if nothing had happened

I walk a road of rust-red earth
perplexed to be here—
early weeks of rainy season,
latitude fifteen south—
on a road about to turn,
come cloudburst at tea-time,
swirl of dust to mudslick

All about blooms bougainvillea,
flamboyants & jacaranda
new maize that now greens
every tillable square inch

Monkeys, up in eucalyptus,
scolding, ask as I do
who I am to be—
crossing woodplank bridge
over month-ago's bone dry
stream-bed now a torrent
splashing waterfall & pool—
where, as warned, I watch
out for mamba snakes

Astounded still at waking up
dawns inside mosquito net
to be twenty-two & walking
somehow this so foreign
mile & half to teach
Achewa & Ngoni kids
history & English,
after lunch, run library

As if in freakish mirror
I see image up ahead
tall above an entourage
of tag-along children,
incongruous & pale:

Pete Nash, BA (Durham)
himself two months out

from south Wales & in
like state of constant startle

headed, after football drills—
throng of pastel-uniformed
Bantu youth in tow,
leading chants of "Stoke City!"—

home to our brick bungalow
with tin roof & sheltered
khonde where we watch
double rainbows at sunset,
eat *nsima*, hear hyenas

Wordless, without nod or wink,
Pete & I, impromptu, passing
break out into "Layla"—

a brief a cappella version
trading off on air-guitar
Duane & Eric's riffs—

astonish assemblage, all of
up-country *boma* in earshot,
into silence a few seconds
before hooted laughter at
azungu craziness—
two white guys gone nuts
to balance strange a bit

Umbrellas then, in unison,
seconds prior to deluge
open up & we,
drenched to skin, resume
quotidian along red dirt road

as if nothing had happened

Feckless, I look on,
safe as thick stone house is

watch from window as
fellow beings batter

captive half a dozen
enemy children

Lull of this afternoon's
siege, I see them

prone by rifle butt
face down, put the boots to

Blood & CS canisters
in ditches flowing past

& I, inured, hardly gag
when pirate "Voice of Peace"

offshore, Middle Sea, somewhere
cues first notes of "Layla"

I curse & weep for species
thru oh-so-lovely coda

Medium wave, from Cyprus, comes
no World Service news, March first

nineteen seventy-nine, common era
of troubles on the West Bank

as if nothing had happened

Good song, "Layla"

The King

(*Biriwiri, Malawi, 8/72*)

Honoured with an audience,
by regal wish about to be
supper guest, a courtier all day,
I sit right hand of throne
chatting with His Majesty
incumbent of Ngoni nation —
kin of Zulu, migrant north

watch supplicants approach
on knees last fifty yards,
hear his Solomonic ruling
in dispute about two cows

inspect, arm-in-arm, a fort
of sun-baked brick, built
for defense of Presbyterians'
mission to heathens & commerce,
of empire against *assegai*
tossed by his ancestors,
over gins & tonic, send up
pommy accents in officers' mess

pass, mid post-prandial walkabout
one of royal consort's *kraal*:
round huts of wattle & daub
chicken coop & bamboo cornrick
fenced by elephant grass,
young girls pounding maize
in mortar with two pestles,
goats that munch on roof thatch

& loudly, blaring off *Nzeru*
short-wave portable from Taiwan
as ubiquitous as cheap—
local brand-name, word for "wisdom"—
we hear old song of young Elvis:
"All Shook Up":

Oh yeah! uhn, uhn, hunh!

Subtropical Homesick Blues
(Ntcheu, Malawi, 12/72)

Mosques & mangoes   full moon drums
six sharp sunsets   winter never comes
Mud is *matope*   *mvula* names the rain

I'll hold you never, love
till back up north again

& I wish Malawi wind
so Arctic wild it blew

that snow flew over Africa
while I lay down with you

Dust & *dambo*   Capricorn stars
flimsy aerogrammes   verses in twelve bars
Heat is *kutentha*   *dzuwa* names the sun

I'll hold you never, love
till down-south time be done

& I wish Malawi wind
so Arctic wild it blew

that ice froze over Africa
while daylight came with you

Angst & aggro   short wave news
sweat-wet sunrise   worn cassettes of blues
Heat is *kutentha*   *mvula* names the rain

I'll leave you never, love
when I get north again

& I wish Malawi wind
so Arctic wild it blew

by magic might from Africa
take me, come dawn, to you

Saturday Night in the Central Region

(Ntcheu, Malawi, 1973)

1   **Number One**

For H.E.'s purple Rolls-Royce
processionals & for
swift passage by Mercedes
Benz of cabinet, there is
"Progress Motorway," the M1:
two aid-swindle asphalt lanes
north-south up from Blantyre's
kickback commerce thru to
H.E.'s new fantastic
capital a-building
in bush about Lilongwe

Courtesy its nearness
Mozambican border,
at halfway point, Ntcheu has
sprung up as a hot spot:
number one for nightlife
hundred miles in all directions

Roadside, prior to moon-rise,
much of Ntcheu passes
along shoulder paths, strewn
with chaff of sugar cane—
all but us invisible, almost

Heedless now & then traffic
we swell onto M1
for progressive mile or so:
past Congress Party HQ
marketplace closed till Monday
post office that boasts only
public phone booth
between Zomba & Dedza
beyond pastel-painted Asian
shops with sun-leached adverts

bound off, all, to various
up-country pleasures:
Saturday night
in the Central Region

H.E., latest palace, slumbers
beside secret consort—
Cecilia, her name is

Foolish scheming ministers
left behind in Lilongwe
plot, incompetently, coups

Off in bush missions, legatees
of Dr. Livingstone stoke
fire for tomorrow's brimstone

Rest of us, cash enough to drink,
beneath intrigue & loosed
from organized religion, join
thirsty march towards
electric beacon up ahead:

string of lights that mimic
Southern Cross, announcing
Megha's Bar has again its
generator up & running

electrics back for stereo
Japanese hi-fi that blasts,
from ways off yet, "Weekend"—
Afro 70s' hottest single—
number one for thousand
miles in all directions:

that, scratch guitar & in
Kiswahili, seven minutes' worth,
praises *"Weeki-yendi-eh,"*

lyrics, best I can make out,
that unto one strange god

give thanks & credit for
whole night thru holy day

so we can forget about
H.E.'s Rolls-Royce & progress,
all together, righteous, get
drunk & under-developed

2   **"The High Life"**

is, by day, a "bottle store,"
selling empties for re-use
Contemplate that

After sunset, as *cantini*
nearest *boma*, it beckons,
thatch roof & white-washed
dry-mud walls by lamplight,
seen but barely, all its
evening bottles, capped & full

Obscure thru oil-lamp
murk & blue tobacco
smoke within are five
tables that all wobble,
three-legged stools & so far
business scant as
frost in a paraffin fridge

Batteries weak, a phonograph
plays offspeed Congolese,
badly-scratched *smanje-manje*

alone to which a scar-faced
Yao up from lakeshore glides
on earthen foot-glossed floor,
adumbrate to complex beat

Off in corner shadows, bargirls
eldest shy of sixteen, jostle
over dibs on two *azungu:*
services to zippered pants,
kwacha from our wallets

A Saturday, bit early yet
for festal customaries
at "The High Life"—

first beer almost cool

3   **Great Rift**

In Megha's courtyard, a spotlight
haloes the proprietor's
ivory, immaculate
'61 Pontiac hardtop

Crowd of those too poor
for bar-price alcohol
guzzles homebrew & dances
to *juju* of Osibisa
off p.a. system for free

Unseen in shadows for minutes
we register ecstatic
swirl of glistening bodies
writhe of rainbow cloth before
start up alarum whispers:
"Azungu! Azungu abwera!"

Warning of "White men come!"
courses celebration's circle
stops dancing dead & turns
on us suspicious eyes
of throng that, deferential, parts
a standing wave of stare & silence

Two hours west by footpath
takes you to brink
of Great Rift Valley,
baboons, orchids, Tarzan vines
Rainforest winds that reach us
come, like tonight,
steamy & reeking of green

Pale & half a foot too tall
still grist for milling curious
we simulate
human gestures, speak
ritual phrases & offer
properly intricate handshakes

Buzz of now distinctly
other tone begins:
"Kaphunzitsi! kaphunzitsi!"

Sussed as "Teachers," we are
now not suspect
European happenstance
the M1 brought—
azungu, yes, but welcome
persons, worthy in our office—
pressed of flesh & quizzes
how-are-you's & where-come-from's

As gallons of *mowa* in gourds
circulate towards us
we brace ourselves for starring
role in passage rites

Mowa is highly authentic
villagers' maize beer
opaque & blood-warm
greyish-beige & drunk
young while brew is
still bubbly in ferment

Alternative test
of mettle & stomach
comes a notch upmarket
from spout of waxed cartons
mowa with imperative
brand name of "Shake-Shake"
enacted dozen times
for extra froth & fizz

Pitch-bending *mbaqanqa*
distortedly pulsates
as we put our mouths
to Africa & swallow

We fit right in,
like a '61 Pontiac
parked beneath papaya tree

4   Black Light

Smuggled in from Mozambique
Megha's black light
bathes all us equally
luminescent & outlandish

Whitewash sweats
as eight-track loops
Percy Sledge & late Jim Reeves

Preening third-class clerks
in polyester radiance
flaunt for would-be consorts

Bargirls' studied leers
read so sullen-eyed fake
lewdness of not-yet women
out this late too early

At table of inebriates
rowdies with month-end
pay-packet *kwacha*
& gaseous lager aplenty,
polyglot shout out abuse

Megha, lugubrious as ever,
tends bar & sees to extras
for police & Congress Party
functionaries of rank

Out on dance floor, a robust
matron fends off automatic
clutches of a toothless
suitor half her size
thwarts with disdain geezer's
laying squeeze to sashay
of *chirundu*-swaddled backside

her wrapcloth print a patriotic
motif of Congress roosters
with visages of stern H.E.
The Life President, Ngwazi
Dr. H. Kamuzu Banda

One icon per ample cheek
syncopated, stereo Kamuzus
jiggle to "Beautiful Sunday"
(*Hey, hey, what a beautiful day!*)

thru-out Commonwealth
Africa a smash hit—
lyrics in English so simple
everyone can sing along:

herself with Himself
a-shimmy on her arse
officious civil servants
constables & thugs
prostitutes & paramours—
goddamn, even Megha—

join in off-key chorus
in basic mother tongue
of resplendent us
azungu, legless drunk
doing the jerk & wa-watusi

Under ultra-violet
& indulgence way off-scale
in drink & dance & song
colour is illusion

In revels of a Saturday
& Sunday's pop-tune praise,
great rifts heal & close
Babel was never built

We are, these nanoseconds,
sisters & brothers
blessedly one species

Reap Time *(5/73)*

Winter's first dust-devils—
spinning vortices
at harvest's close,
auguries of drought—
whirl thru Ntcheu this noon

Last night, late, between
window lattices came
stench of surfeit mangoes,
left on branches, rotten
&, on chillest breezes yet,
battery of *gule* drums
syncoptic to the season

There, with luck, will be
for Achewa & Ngoni
maize enough not to starve
before December's capricious
rains, perhaps, return
over low mountains
back from Mozambique

Yield of own year is
notes towards bad novel,
sheaves of paper, scribbled on

If to ancient rhythms
I ever am to dance
raise voice up to song
harmonious of substance
with grain or two of truth

this May must I slash
with recall's sickle &
acutest pen, cut
stooks of iffy harvest:

to reap, you sow

Solar *(12/73)*

All that winter's train, midnight
local, westbound, out of Montréal
I am wanton after sun

—that sun, but year ago & us then
aboard steamship "Ilala," burning
rust-red, down on Lake Nyasa—

Outside Brockville, bored so stiff
December endless hour, wait on
hitch-up of Ottawa shuttle

—that sun, blazen, sear & beaches
languid, beside rest house, under
cottonwood groves, Nkota-kota—

Whistle, air-brake, clouds of steam
ice on steel, mesh some, miss some:
Kingston, Belleville, Trenton

—that sun, gleam so clear & fathoms
deep, splendid skin-dive sparkles
rainbow fishes off Salima—

Moon-glints, lakeshore ice-sheets
swaying trestle, sleet & stark stubble:
Cobourg, Port Hope, Oshawa

—that sun, tangerines & baobab
fish eagle, lizard giant, jacaranda
sun by local name, that *dzuwa*—

Dawn twice bleak, so Union Station
tunnel, subway, rental attic room
where waits, stamp African, her letter

—that sun, by aerogramme, new come
sweat, dust & spices, arisen sub-tropics
northerly now shines, as, twilight dawn

I, solacious in Toronto, spinning
worn LP record, sit by dormer sill
beam, transported, to old Beatles' tune:

"Here comes... Here comes...
Here comes   (click!) the sun"

.

IV

Ground Goes Figure

Wind Instrument

(for James C. Ison)

Once upon a great lake
sloop with full sail set
Toronto-bound & borne
off to truths unsought
Ison at helm & I
now less queasy posit
Einstein was a sailor
out on open waters where
space is waves
& time is liquid

Come about
off Grimsby spit
port is left in plural
senses & semantics
from landlock let loose

Jib set, sheets taut
jenny out, we make
four knots, north-northwest
as thought free-floats
& words play thru
lacustrine changes:
Ground goes figure
fathoms beyond
physics gale force meta

Listen Ison says & I
learn to navigate by ear:
proper trim & bearing
true course making
both best speed & sound
keen melody of wind
that alto sings thru sheets
descants over sailcloth
hums continuo on keel

& Charlie Parker, man
he'd be fantastic
cat at tiller under canvas
old salt at impromptu
navigation, wind control
spontaneous at instrument
Dizzy, deft as first mate
cheeky on turns at task
billowing breezes to tune
Coltrane for longer blows

Darwin, as we know
truly was a sailor
knew from Beagle's voyage
that human body is
an earthly vessel but
adaptable to water
given time & need for
weather eye & sea legs
knew that by degree
equilibrium evolves

Once out on that great lake
by mid-crossing, unthinking
you flex with familiar
yaw & pitches, feel
fifteen marks off-centre
as if on kilter (& will
back on terra firma
stumble first few steps)

CN Tower as our beacon
intent on harbour pleasures
I at tiller feel secure
smug almost to ken
newly so much nautical
lore until thermals off
swelter of city blast us

heave us starboard hard
over till we take on
water & I panic:
revert to landlubber

useless as Ison reefs
jib & mainsail &
docks safely at marina

Twice to cross this great lake
morning next & chastened
deckhand barely able
we shove off south-east, set
course for Niagara
mouth of river where
no winds want to take us
but by frequent oblique tack

Capricious blow these breezes
until midday when they die
fetch us, becalmed, up
bobbed by swell all afternoon
adrift mid-lake
where garbage gathers

Apt passages from Homer
sagas & Coleridge come
Anglo-Saxon curses
as we strike our luffing
useless sails

prime, pull on & pray over
puny outboard
putt-putt
thence to Grimsby
earth & stanzas of lesson—

Warning to all craft:
prevailing winds are fickle

Beware
uncharted metaphors

The tiller is
an instrument of music

Come-from-Away

(for Stan Rogers)

Stan, well, he was every inch
& never much a sailor

Bold-faced, baritone & shameless
Stan pure lied about
knowing of those boats
so many them named after women:

from pulled up, rotten dories
through *Bluenose* & her sister
that one-lung Cape Islander
old, sound still but, & kindly
fleets of collier, turtleback & whaler
his last-run great lake steamer
all those sloops & schooners
all but vessels for his craft

I take no little comfort
telling truths on Stan Rogers
himself from down same road
also, by birth, but "come-from-away"
made up by wile with words

Because, damn, so many women
I could name share deeply
strange regard I'm jealous of
for that huge, bald & bearded,
bold-faced baritone & shameless
pure lying son of a bitch

(apologies to mother Valerie)

I, in smallness of spirit, relish
muchly widow Ariel's account
of turn at wheel of *Bluenose*
the replica, of course, which
after couple minutes, ends, has
Stan green & tossing lunch

I wish that I had had that
tale to tattle then, so to bear
on home to her, she earliest:

she who wore out gift,
signed copy of *Fogarty's Cove*,
its first release on vinyl,
played nothing else, for weeks

she, who made me Maui shirt
so loud, Stan, backstage
Gage Park festival, suggests
switch for volume control

I must, being honest, now confess
shame at pettiness, here—
obvious to yet another
of the Stan-besotted,
her I love & live with:

she, for whom I sought out
bought, on compact disc
his works, complete, her birthday
she, nonetheless, who mostly plays
"Mary Ellen Carter," over & over again

must, along with this calumnious
giveaway of secret, expose
myself as neither much a sailor:

tell, how, offered helm, once
of C&C thirty-three footer
her mast off for repair
under diesel inboard
somewhere on Conception Bay, I

a come-from-away, like idiot
chasing far-off whales, within
blunders of a couple minutes
fouled her prop round buoy-line
belongs to somebye's lobster trap

how for, deplorable, my sins
our St. John's hosts, no choice
had to radio the Coast Guard
whose guys, despite survival suits
after brisk submersions to untangle
frayed rope from prop, serious
froze, got right pissed off

With these Newfoundlanders
after, so embarrassed; I
in chagrin myself, in galley
hunkered down & tossing jars, decide
time has come to fess up

admit, as they suspect already
their expenses-paid freelance
mainland magazine writer
here to research supplement
flacking cod & Newfoundland

does not, never ever, eat fish,
any food that swam or came from
life spent under water, not
on a dare nor even to keep up,
blown now anyway, my crafty cover; add

how I rig up ad hoc substitute
for lobsterman's lost marker
with four litre jug, emptied
but late of truly bad Chablis; insist

how absence swells need
to invent perfect mother; cite
example of Stan Rogers
himself but even worse a sailor—
fine old salt at song's own helm

call upon imaginary powers
summon down on anxious waters
somewhere on Conception Bay, I
made up by wile with words

I shall, subsequent & largely, tell
truth on us both to all his women:

she, with boy's name & the boy
who sings "Barrett's Privateers"
best of anyone; she for whom
I, scummy, pirated whole canon
one Christmas, next year had to
dub another for her sister

With same purpose want to say
to women such & also to that guy
survived his oil-rig sinking
out in North Atlantic by singing
"Mary Ellen Carter," over & over again

(sometime, I think, late spring
of '83, just about when
in fluke fire & thinnest air
out of assumed element
aboard wrong sort vessel
down on Cincinnati tarmac
same time Stan did not)

hope to say, as Stan's survivors
let us all rejoice
that metaphors are ocean stars
to steer by deadly reckon
do allow for reach of the lie
that songs perhaps may
come from away:

from, sometimes, us, or other sort
any huge, bald & bearded,
bold-faced baritone & shameless
pure lying son of a bitch

(no apologies, necessity, you mother)

every inch, hell—
none us need be sailor

Bet Against the Dealer

(for Ian Tyson)

Loudly optimistic, largish fellow
stands up, inhales, fully
quarter-mile from stage—
annoying all about—
hollers for "Summer Wages"
Damned if, straight off, that is
not tune Tyson plays

Cargo cults get started like this:
a fluke of crowd hush
& favour of breezes
so bellow gets heard
passes over stoney ground
from prayer to answer

A devotee might just
misconstrue coincidence
as blessing only due
a faith goes way way back
to Vanguard vinyl
to "Pissy," "Maude" & autoharp
Mr. Spoons & learning
chords to "Four Strong Winds"

Pompous ass, he sits
holding ace & king & wishes
that his all-time favourite—
"Irving Berlin (Is a Hundred Yrs Old Today)"—
had a shorter title

wishes on aurora borealis
that he, too, had had
old chestnut for Neil Young
to cover &, off that,
roped in royalties enough for
deposit on ranch & a half-ton
some to see winter thru

is not so foolish as to
ante up for horses

Noises Off: A Found Poem

(for Glenn Gould & Foster Hewitt)
from *The Globe and Mail* (12/11/93):

"CBC Radio editor
Peter Cook and engineer
Don Davies were
remastering
some early Gould recordings
recently
for a new CD
to be released this month
when a voice spoke:
Here in the first period…
it's in the corner…
out front to Sawchuk.

A hockey game,
as described by Hewitt, had
somehow
inserted itself into
a 1955 broadcast
from Massey Hall
of Gould's rendition of
Bach's *Keyboard Concerto in D Minor*
with the Toronto Symphony.

The explanation is
a technical one. Davies
had so successfully
'de-noised'
the original Gould recording
that radio
interference
of the day was
now audible.

It turns out that night,
as Gould was broadcasting
live from Massey Hall

the Maple Leafs were playing
the Detroit Red Wings…
just a few blocks north….

They lost 3 - 0."

Off the Wall

I need first address your disbelief

Rational as I, you shall
suspect what follows
to be—if not a lie—
tricked up for poem's sake

Nonetheless, fact is:
on May morning, '81
came news of Marley's death
I found small picture frame
had fallen off
alcove wall to hardwood
shattered glass, face up
his photograph beneath

I warned you, yes

An eyewitness, I, & I am
yet of two minds

Cover of a magazine, this was
an iconic Marley:
tight to face, eyes-on
coils of smoke
from mighty spliff
swirl like exhaled dreadlocks

red, black, gold & green
graphic motifs
caption in boldest font:
"This man is seeing God!"

Coincidence, of course:
a happenstance in synch
of cancer & loose nail
events remote by more than just
few thousand miles of distance

Keen I am on Occam's razor
mindful p's & Q.E.D. — But

deep right hemisphere, there is
unmapped fold or crevice
for processes of prophecy
biochemistry of faith

synapses that fire off
all psalms & ceremonies
prehistory thru present
defying utter randomness:

Great Rift hunt-dreams
handprints upon cave wall
testaments & temples
vedas, sagas, suras
outer edge of astrophysics

Hard-wired to mystic, we are
disposed as a species
to go for hocus-pocus

to act on coded urge
to find in broken glass
manifest signs
cosmic fractals that mark
passing of Bob Marley

be open to miraculous
receptive at our cells

Innate will to sing
Zion song in Babylon
has us praise & celebrate
spiritus mundi that we
sense at electron level

to harmonize chaos
to be magic

get not a little spooked
when whatever knocks
icons down off wall

leaves behind the smell of
something funny in the room

Apollo *(20/7/69)*

"The lunatic, the lover, and the poet,
Are of imagination all compact."
                    —*A Midsummer-Night's Dream* V, i

I raced Eagle to the moon
that Sunday in July
on earth & 401
eastbound with Acadian
compact's pedal floored
pushing almost 80
mundane mph

escaping past weekend's
visit all gone wrong
with I-forget-which girlfriend—
in Guelph, perhaps Stratford—

lust cut short & I
crazily thereafter pushing
car-radio buttons
hot after history, catch
famous, now, first words:

Hello, Houston:
Tranquility Base
The Eagle has landed

receive, static-free
message, crest of 4-lane
pass thru blasted limestone
west of Gananoque

lose by less than hundred
miles compensatory
private mad space race

exhale with Walter Cronkite & a
bunch of guys
turning blue

I arrive on fumes
am at rec-room tv
buzzed for several hours
before, at last, Neil Armstrong

in grainy chiaroscuro
descends Eagle's lunar
lander ladder & screws up:

That's one small step
for [...] man
One giant leap
for mankind

Months he must have thought
what words to speak—
first human to touch foot
on surface not of earth—
& he blew it:

spoke, in stumble, with
the indefinite
article left out

Spoke without that *a*—
that mundane, ordinary *a*
Armstrong's meant-to-be
propitious words—
misspoke, but as all remember—
lack a gravity
fail utterly to leap

Man on the moon!
Man on the moon!

Apollo is the sun god

Poetry is in the details

Satellite Observations

This then, when only one
channel was & snowy
supper-hour weather
forecasts included
time & quadrant best to
spot new satellites

important enough stuff
to have us: Mom & Dad
& bundled two kids up
way past bedtime keeping
winter backyard vigil for
twinkles tracking slowly
low off south horizon

Here now, I have no
access to my seven-
year-old's fascination,
few details but these:
"sputnik" a funny word,
concern about that
orbiting dog,
a kindergarten tune
I did not know as Mozart

Next then, ten, eleven,
planet's whirl about our sun
to weirdness of a summer
sophomoric Sunday
afternoon with tv set
on to warm up tubes

(same Admiral on swivel
base from stanzas above
hauled along to undergrad
years of supper-hour
Star Trek reruns)

hunk of black hash & us
as sci-fi becomes fact

By inaugural beams
of global broadcast
via comsat, we
watch, as credits roll,
a child that instant
being born in Mexico

go, live link, shortly after
to Abbey Road & witness
Beatles et al. recording
"All You Need Is Love"

Pictures a bit fuzzy

This last, a fine & balmy
night in '90s June
with solar circuitry
geared for total eclipse
of Earth's first satellite—

such a show of our
planet's passing thus
between sun & moon
not likely to rerun
in times of any now alive—

event to start at ten

Cosmic lookout
kept by candleglow
glasses frosty
garden aromatic
deck chairs, east-south-east

nigh on syzygy,
at cast of earth as
crescent shadow,
neighbours' two kids flee:
opt for indoors &
weather-channel version

Picture perfect
no songs

Famous First Notes

(for Barry Keith Grant)

Play, please, some jazz
I might like, you think

So, those fateful words
to Dr. Grant put, off-hand

As I spoke, perhaps
dozen altered years ago
winter sunshine broke
dumb resistance deeper
than snow it also melted
all about in countryside
us, out by Fifth Louth:

Simple, he says, straight off
pulls from shelf & cues
vinyl answer got himself
dozen other years before

in Manhattan somewhere
in innocence, same request
put to now lost-track-of friend
already fan of that jazz stuff:

& not so long ago, Rob Nunn
as we listen to cassette version
his sabbatical flat, in Montréal
catch-up talk in second tongue

tells how in Berkeley same track
was, off jukebox, laid on him
likewise, dozen years before ours
plus ça change, plus la même chose:

says also but last week how
he heard on FM jazz show
host Katie Malloch recollect
her capture by this music, cite
first cut, same '59 release:

So in synch this feels:
all four times, four/four,
famous, those first notes

by sextet, solid, resonant
key of D minor, mesh
linking four far-flung
friends to long-gone places

Thus four times, forever
these attuned, their subsequent
recorded music collections
all by jazz to be augmented:

Dig this, man! said then
is heard again, each time over
over three decades after
our world so much wider

now, digital, on CD
re-mastered, enter Paul
Chambers's string bass
& Bill Evans's piano
intro dialogue, before
trumpet of Miles Davis
John Coltrane on tenor,
Cannonball on alto sax
& Cobbs's drums come in:

"So What," this is

whisper four voices, reverb
famous first notes, as
whole universe spins out
kind of new

V

Instrumental to Our Planet

Armstrong's Cornet

It lies in silent state—
tacky sideshow
tourist New Orleans:

draped with his white handkerchief
between its valves & bellow

baffed, its tubing
nearest mouthpiece bent

brass in several places worn
by touch & play of fingers, silver

Garish, in dissonance
hang, gilt-framed, on wall behind
1930s vintage showbills:

left, your "Satchmo," clownish
muggin' fo' de white folks

wrong, a bow-tied "Lou-ie" jaunts
as jewelled pun, his coronet

Not so, not on off-blue
plastic-glued-on-plywood daïs
chief lure to cheap museum

no, no, by any justice
Armstrong's cornet
ought to be enshrined

alongside Leonardo's
goose quill & oily brushes
with Galileo's stolen scope
next to Einstein's blackboard

Louis's device, no less
instrumental to our planet—

without which
it does not swing

Another Day at the Office

Listen closely as Louis
tosses off his third
master track since lunch—

Los Angeles, late fall
1957
sessions for Verve
pick of songbook
vocals mostly gig with
trio & young Oscar—

 listen to a has-been
"mouldy fig" called "Pops"
sing for scale & posterity
business-hours
masterpieces

Without hit for ages
"Satchmo," at fifty-seven
gets movie cameos
& low-bill clownish
tv guest spots
does casinos, fronts
State Department tours

thirty years now since
Hot 5 & 7
records define jazz—
white handkerchief
& "muggles" smile—has
minor role in show biz

Listen, as Louis voices
with ease, liberties
sounded first on cornet
over 1920s
roar of Chicago

earns an overcast
Tuesday's wages

Hear how Cole Porter's
"I Get A Kick" gets
on first verse's last phrase
surprise sibilants—

catch, next turnaround
two-bar phrase
spontaneous scat

hear, second verse, Louis
hie up melodic
mimetics to
apropos heights—

for all four-plus minutes'
entirety of keeper
first take, effortless
swing Peterson, Brown
Ellis & Bellson

Armstrong's vocal, as if
plenty's horn of brass
rasping, soaring
smears & polishes

chorus after chorus, spans
Great White Way
to Congo Square
champagne to Jax & corn
whiff of Storyville reefer

by late day's second wind
ad libs magnetic
reels of ordinary tape
into excellence, waxes
ephemera that last

Listen, lucky us, as
Louis performs office

Account of Basie

Esteem give Freddie Green
who five decades so well
strums four to bar
on archtop solid chords
never ever cheats

Jo Jones, drums, just applause
righteous Walter Page
string bass, likewise:
standout rhythm tandem
twenty years in synch

Plaudits to hotshot horns:
young Lester leaping in
Buck, Herschel, Sweets
head charts, jump & jive-ass
Jimmy Rushing shouts

Acclaim as Count Basie
orchestrates & places
punctuation
Jersey stride, K.C. style
blues, clean down to bone:

"One o'clock," one more time:
chitlin' circuit dance halls
bandstands, bus rides
ten-inch Decca singles
radio, Savoy

Boogie-woogie, V-discs
rabbit stew to match-set
silk tuxedos
"Atomic," Las Vegas
"April in Paris"

Streamline locomotive
superannuated:
Count in wheelchair
ghost band gigs, four to bar
swings till his last breath

The Duke Suite

1   **Fingertip Traces**

Young Master Ellington had
earliest classes with
piano teacher who rejoiced in
name of Mrs Clinkscales,
hated, at seven, finger exercises
skipped off lessons for baseball

Adolescent Edward had,
before out of school, for
stylish duds & put-on manners,
been graced with title "Duke"

has, late teens, a day-job
painting signs & fronts
rough diamond ragtime band
that gets odd Saturday gigs
at 50 cents per man

Two years less young, & wiser,
Ellington in parents' parlour
seeks out mastery,
chooses as his mentor
James P. Johnson's
"Carolina Shout"
in performance by composer
as recorded onto
perforated roll of paper

slows pianola mechanism,
making keys depress
half-speed, Duke traces
moving sounds with other

places fingertips on paradigm,
faithful second-hand,
duets as disciple

Quite a piece of work
Duke picked himself
to be second teacher:

three strains that intertwine
in sections, syncopated
choruses of 16 bars—
left hand tricky, right no cinch:

"Carolina Shout"—
first solo jazz on record,
esteemed in all the best
coloured speaks up eastern
seaboard north to Harlem

James P.'s shibboleth
"Carolina Shout" was,
serving all thru 20s roar
as piano rite of passage:

not just in title resonant
of darkest deep south slavery
where, come sabbath, massas
tolerated worship
means of "ringshouts"—
raucous circle dances,
African in jubilance:

suborned old rites' stomp
of field-hard feet, translating
plantation Sundays' church floors
into freedom's drum—

thru stride piano come
opportune to Washington
D.C. front parlour where
new-determined tyro,
daily defter, places fingers

erudite on pulse of
percussive legacy & *the*
idiorhythmic talent

"To be a great bull-shitter is great, but to be a great bull-shitter and wear a diffusing veneer over the bullshit is the ultimate."
— Duke Ellington

"Tone parallel":
an Ellingtonic coinage
for suites & feats orchestral
mimetic titular subject:

Colours:
spectrum's swirl of hues:
skin-shades, dark to lesser so
blue modes & moody tinctures
pastels to translucence:

Moments:
solid time, in swing, suspended:
preludes, hep to possible
moot aperçus & second's linger
essential as perfume:

Places:
Harlem as his epicentre,
jazz topography writ vast:
itinerary's spin of planet's ball
Afro-Far-East-Euro-Latin:

People:
biographic aural sketches of
creole beauties, Bojangles, Ella,
his & Shakespeare's players
Kings, Balthazar to Martin Luther:

"Tone parallel":
an Ellingtonic coinage
for ultimate in such sweet
bullshit they only let
geniuses get away with

3   **Loved You Madly**

Tuxedo, grin & brilliantine
gloss over bitterness:

At Cotton Club, announcer
saying *Now, the boys'll*
play that jungle music

Tone-deaf managers extorting
co-composer credits

Dixie tour Pullman cars,
service entrances & lunch
counters with no service

Trombonist Juan Tizol
blackfaced for Hollywood

At secrecy of other
mistress, after music,
because she was white

Forty years, a thousand works
too little for a Pulitzer

Nadir of summer '55
in Flushing, New York:
six weeks second billing
to ice skates & water show

For rest of his life,
with mustachio'd smile
Duke, *con brio*, demurs:

I was born in 1956
at the Newport festival

4   **Synergy**

Duke & Billy Strayhorn
early days of Billy's dying

two coasts dislocated
anxious to start composing
first of *Sacred Concerts*

over phone agree on
precise initial task:
write, overnight, six notes
for text of *Genesis* 1:
"In the beginning, God...."

Duke & Billy Strayhorn
as per longtime practice—
tho never quite like this
a continent apart—
small hours at pianos
had, by dawn, six notes each:

melodies that both
start off F natural
& finish at A flat—
four notes out of six
same pitch, exact order

5   **"Black Butterfly"**
     (for Warren Stirtzinger)

Protocol of jazz has
hippest request be
that player call next tune:
perhaps an obscure gem
fingers itch to fondle

Advisor on these matters—
tweed jacket & loud tie
solo gig at lunch-time
downtown doomed café
Friday of a too-long winter—
gives, on Gibson archtop,
readings, book of Duke:

tasty boppish takes on
medley of the usuals & then—
returning nod of single
patron come to listen—
plays this gorgeous thing:

bittersweet & surely
vintage Ellington but not
ever one I recognize—
not by eight bars in
not after entire chorus

Thinking that when set ends
I must ask Warren what
tune it was I called

I glance out frosted window
where neon of newly-open
mission to the homeless
proclaims Jesus Lord

& I, in hippest silence,
request spring

Pictures of Billie

Prelude

If hope to conjure up
music, means of mere words, be
dim as dancing architecture
how more so to eulogise

singer thru her photographs
to gaze upon jazz thus
& so strike tacit notes
voice counterpoint I see

Spite of all, as I peruse
various pictures of Billie,
houses sway in fancy steps

synaesthesia happens:
smoky air tastes bittersweet
resounds of white gardenia

Appropriated Blues, Stanza 1

A coloured girl, mister, ain't got no horn
Said—coloured girl, baby, ain't got no horn
Shuckin' that jive since day I's born

Gardenia Profile

Hand-tinted, this enhancement
of pre-war photo graces
deluxe box set's cover—
agency's new promo shot
of nascent star with trademark:

She, in profile, downcasts
half her face in shadow

chin to silky shoulder parallel
camera angled such that
eyes show, irises all but black

Her skin, at twenty-some, flawless
"high brown," luminescent
her lips, fuller than fashion
then drew lipstick edges,
deepest dark of red
Look where cleft at nostrils
catches beam of spotlight
& there on upper lip
insistence of her embouchure
beneath a bruise of paint

Teardrop arch of brow,
plucked & penciled
golden hoop in earlobe
eyelids indigo & silver
her hair as waves of jet
pulled loosely up & pinned
Rakish, high of temple
there is, of course, a grand
corsage of white gardenia

Heartstop beautiful:
tristesse in youthful smoulder
posed as contrapuntal to
dewy, glossy cool of those
partly-furled-yet blossoms
rapt by secrets, poised
taut as a two-bar break

Let us go to nightclub stage:
call up quartet with Prez
have Billie at our request,
paused thru turnaround,
about to sing any old phrase
with "baby" in it, say
"All of Me," last verse—why not?

Appropriated Blues, Stanza 2

No-good songs; turn 'em right t' gold
Sad-assed song, turn it bright & gold
Get me to Harlem cuz my bones is cold

Carnegie Hall & Long Gloves

Caught in shutter-flash by press
photog from downstage off
she, on verge of entrance
stage right, under draped velvet,
hesitates when hears
standing ovation she dreads

At thirty-three & in disguise
turned out chaste as debutante
Billie in frilly tafetta, a white
floor-length layered gown,
demurely décolletée,
shoulder ruffles, sleeveless
pearl choker & long gloves
white silk well past elbows

Lady Day, as if about to curtsy,
clutches fast her skirt, gainsays
hauteur in tilt of head
reveals, as false, fixed smile.
Terrified, she thinks
perhaps to herself whispers:
They've come to see the scars

(As that new-then old joke goes:
A tourist in Manhattan comes
up to bunch of jazz musicians,
cool, just hanging out, & asks
How do you get to Carnegie Hall?
They, in chorus, answer: *Practice, man!*)

Billie's answer's not so funny:
first, listen, really listen, to Louis,

to Bessie on gramophone next door
scrub clean white folks' steps

from age thirteen, turn tricks & sing
sing damned any song as if
worthy life's last breath

Out of Tin Pan Alley's
garbage pluck pure gems
register southern bus-tour
indignities of roadside pisses,
service entrances to ballrooms

Suffer cracker taunts
& love of liberals, be
boffo smash at hippest cafés,
fear for your cabaret card

Pearl, with cast of low-life
swine in Harlem late-night,
spike up hardest stuff

Screw them! Screw Carnegie Hall!
Sing your fuckin' ass off!

Sing the scars they've
come to see

God bless you, child,
grown-up, got your own

Appropriated Blues, Stanza 3

Smack dab men, you mess wid my heart
Smack dab men, hot veins to my heart
Oh, sweet Daddy, gotta shoot me your dart

Strange Fruit

By glamour stylings, I'd guess
early 50s: more, by far, of her
less, some say, of voice

Gone thru strung-out gaunt
past arrests & lifted card
court-ordered cure, taken twice

Billie here is sassy plump,
a Norman Grantz production
European first-class tours
Gershwin, Porter et al. stuff
for Lady Day records, at last

Above blue-dyed feather boa,
almost face-on, her mouth
pursed, smallish scarlet
nostrils flared, eyelids shut,
their metallic makeup matching
large pearl on lobe,
she is all pro & polished
showbiz as should be—so?

So pure lilt has up & gone?
Surprise & upper octave lost?
Technique, there's technique
drink, & a track record

Previous song, last of set,
by weary rote now, seeking
whereabouts of latest lover scum

she will, as encore, do
her famous southern ditty:
by audience request,
sing a song of lynching

Appropriated Blues, Stanza 4

Calls me "Lady Day," man who does me good
Calls me "Lady Day," man who does me good
Crazy, way he loves me—how I wish he could!

Fine & Mellow

On kinescope, this picture moves:

Ungainly bulk of television
camera tight on Billie's
1957 face, front-lit,
skin grainy nearest shadows
grooves that deepen when she smiles
as, assuredly, she does
perched on studio stool,
focus of selectest circle:
Ben Webster, Coleman Hawkins
Eldridge, white kid Mulligan
Jo Jones, so on & Prez

In flickering clip, we glimpse her
hair by elastic bound up,
loose at back to shoulders,
no makeup, slacks & sweater
as if at singer's dream rehearsal
wise eyes wide open, smiling,
almost forty & clean

Already Holiday has sung
two blues choruses she wrote
as if changes I-IV-V
had, that instant, been discovered
as if that day on slave ship
pentatonic scale first rattled chains
as if, just this early morning,
lovers turned out unfaithful

Now, almost even better
we get to see her listen
listen to Lester's solo &
altho silent, sing duet

drinking deep thru very pores
Prez's tenor sax
that sound, as always was—
strange & sure, oblique as light—
her soul's other voice

I love you, Billie Holiday
here, as by electrons' flow
to cathode tube & screen,
you articulate each nuance
of Prez's improv, show
exact sense of unheard words
out of fleetest glances
stunning music make

By subtle nod & wrinkle flaunt
flick of brow, a shrug, a sway
by delicious lick of lip
Billie, you, so lovely,
mute, but singing

Out-Chorus

There is no photograph
for this:

In hospital deathbed
New York narcs

planted white junk
busted her black ass

Taped to left calf
of Billie's corpse

101

a nurse, her fan, found
Holiday's stash:

in small bills,
about a hundred bucks

Thelonious: A Quintet for Monk

1   **"Misterioso"**

Zenith of summer
at almost tomorrow

kitchen door & windows
open wide as by

behest random breezes
gift of wind chimes

tuned to blue notes
counterpoise Thelonious

solo in San Francisco

A duet by serendip

more than forty minutes plays
out under lucky stars

tempered metal tubes at
random swinging

syncopate to ivory

A miracle it was:
round about midnight

when here there was
no one else

to hear with me as Monk
jams with universe

in '59 & present tense
perfectly in sync

so *misterioso*

2   "Smoke Gets in Your Eyes"

One by squirming one
half of evening class

by twist of face
& screw of body so much
more eloquent than tongues

pronounces
verdict not in favour
rejects this as unjust:

condemns Monk
his hammering pop
tune into dissonance
as concerto
way too, way too weird

Most, thus far
out from easy listen
comfort come
reluctantly

more, at every note
now contort & swear
goddamns
at modern jazz

not quite soon enough

Well before his quintet has
done with Jerome Kern

Thelonious, he has them
cringe, as if

smoke got
into ears

3   **"Epistrophy"**

Tough gig
it's got to be
eccentric

a genius but somehow
off

assuming most
bizarre of hats

Hear sour minor
notes as sweet

If necessary, bend
pianos, be

connoisseur of curious
words like
'crepuscule'

Know whatever
'epistrophy' means

Never let your
socks match

4   **"Ruby, My Dear"**

She, our amaryllis
under skylight, overdue
gift since Christmas, this

rare & brilliant
February afternoon
labours to unfurl

minute-by-minute pushes
full-scale into bloom

She permits me
privilege of watching

to listen as she calls
upon Thelonious
Sphere Monk's abject
paean to his wife

as select score for her
birthing of blossom

He to baptise red
radiant petals
rubato in rubineous

striking piano music

5   "Abide With Me"

After, godless, I die
when whatever obsequies
be done & spoke, please
remember I will need
"Abide With Me"—
Monk's arrangement
with Hawkins & Coltrane
both glorious on tenor—
fifty-two sanctified
seconds' worth

Twice at bit too loud
ought to be holy
enough to cover if
best bets turn out wrong

I will want a proper wake:
houseful of friends
song & smoke & whisky
overflowing into garden
intercessory till dawn
pints of fathomless ale
ordinary wine from cellar
drunk to emptiness

If there be at that
far off, I hope, event
sadness at my death, desist

Read aloud instead those few
better poems I left about
how blessed it is
on such day as this
in full to be alive —

Monk's music & magic
words at fingertips

Please do remember why
I called this tune

Terrance Cox lives in St. Catharines, Ontario. He performs his own poems to musical accompaniment on the recently released spoken word CD, *Local Scores*. His work has also appeared in numerous journals, including *Dalhousie Review, Grain, The Fiddlehead, Prism International, Quarry* and *Queen's Quarterly*. This is his first book.

AGMV Marquis

MEMBER OF SCABRINI MEDIA

Quebec, Canada
2001